peaceful christmas
piano solos

a collection of 30 pieces

ISBN: 978-1-5400-5580-4

Visit Hal Leonard Online at
www.halleonard.com

Contact Us:
Hal Leonard
7777 West Bluemound Road
Milwaukee, WI 53213
Email: info@halleonard.com

In Europe contact:
Hal Leonard Europe Limited
42 Wigmore Street
Marylebone, London, W1U 2RN
Email: info@halleonardeurope.com

In Australia contact:
Hal Leonard Australia Pty. Ltd.
4 Lentara Court
Cheltenham, Victoria, 3192 Australia
Email: info@halleonard.com.au

Angels from the Realms of Glory

Words by James Montgomery
Music by Henry T. Smart

Auld Lang Syne

Words by Robert Burns
Traditional Scottish Melody

Away in a Manger

Traditional
Words by John T. McFarland (v.3)
Music by William J. Kirkpatrick

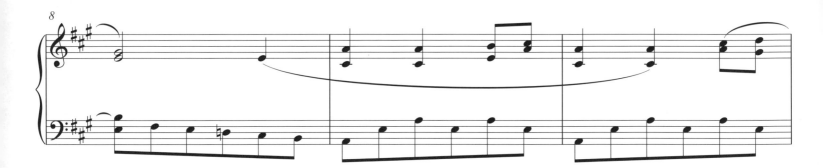

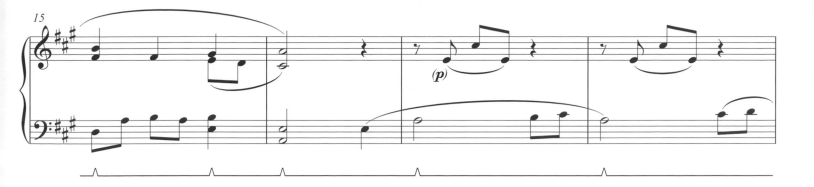

Blue Christmas

Words and Music by Billy Hayes and Jay Johnson

Bring a Torch, Jeannette, Isabella

17th Century French Provencal Carol

Christmas Lights

Words and Music by Guy Berryman, Will Champion, Chris Martin and Jonny Buckland

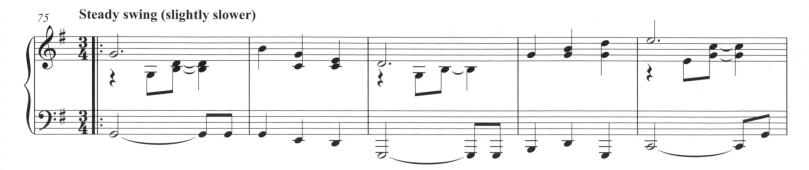

Steady swing (slightly slower)

A tempo, meno mosso

straight quavers

pp

Coventry Carol

Traditional Carol

The First Noel

17th Century English Carol
Music from W. Sandys' Christmas Carols

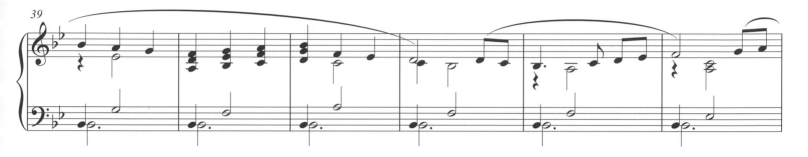

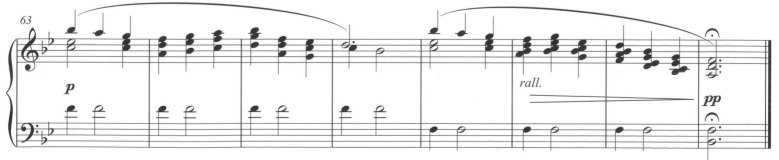

Glow

from *World of Color Winter Dreams*

Words and Music by Eric Whitacre

Have Yourself a Merry Little Christmas

from *Meet Me in St. Louis*

Words and Music by Hugh Martin and Ralph Blane

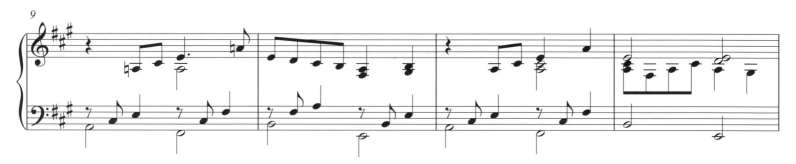

The Holly and the Ivy

18th Century English Carol

Moderately slow Gospel groove ♩ = 80

To Coda

30

CODA

molto rit.

(There's No Place Like) Home for the Holidays

Words and Music by Al Stillman and Robert Allen

Brightly ♩ = 60

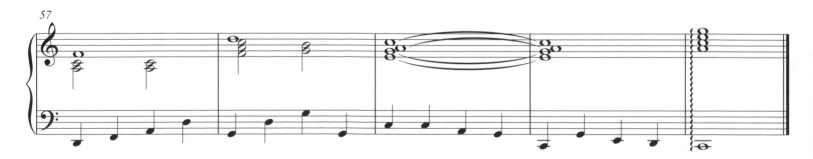

I Heard the Bells on Christmas Day

Words by Henry Wadsworth Longfellow
Music by John Baptiste Calkin

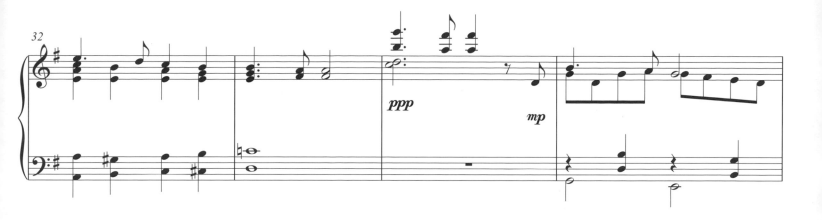

I Wonder as I Wander

By John Jacob Niles

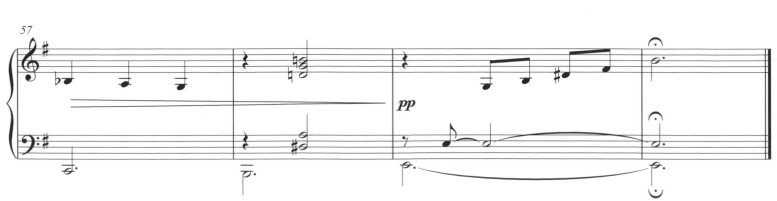

In the Bleak Midwinter

Poem by Christina Rossetti
Music by Gustav Holst

Gradually slowing

It Came Upon the Midnight Clear

Words by Edmund H. Sears
Traditional English Melody
Adapted by Arthur Sullivan

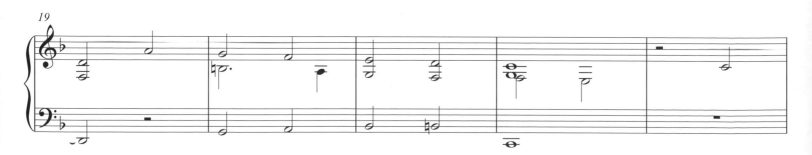

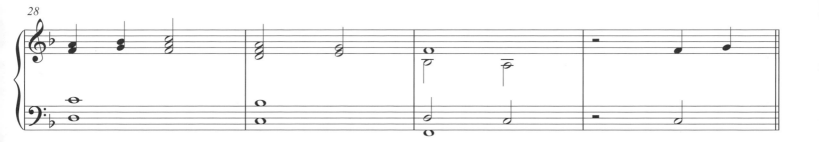

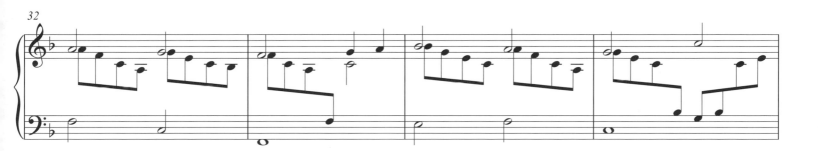

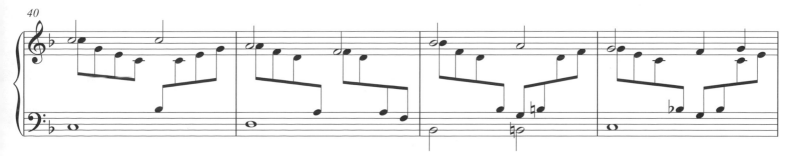

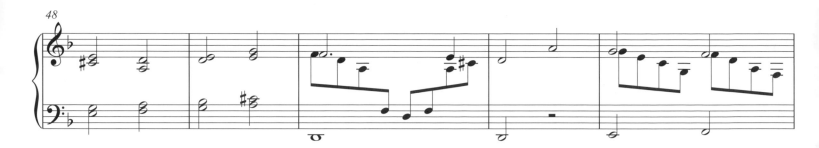

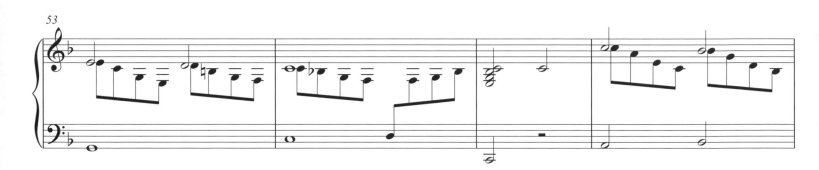

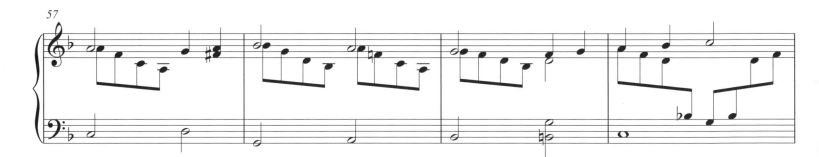

It's Beginning to Look Like Christmas

By Meredith Willson

Moderate Swing ♩ = 80

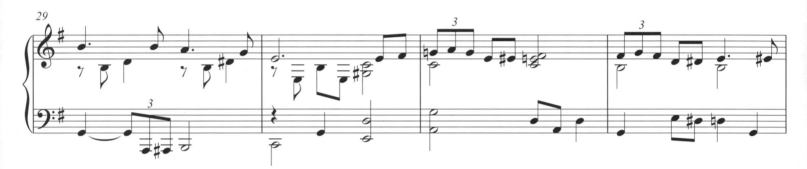

D.S. al Coda

CODA

49

Let It Snow! Let It Snow! Let It Snow!

Words by Sammy Cahn
Music by Jule Styne

swung eighths

straight eighths

8va

sub. **pp**

The Most Wonderful Time of the Year

Words and Music by Eddie Pola and George Wyle

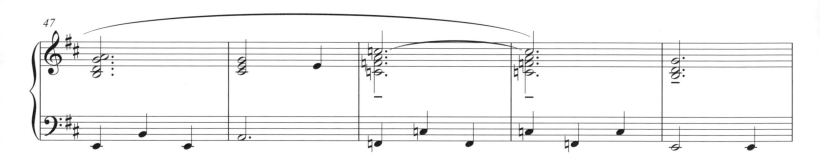

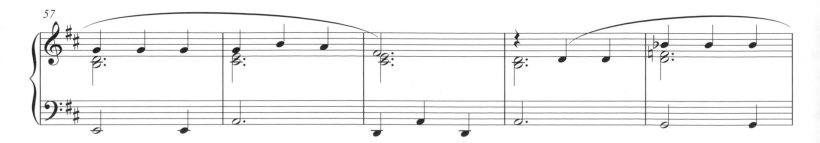

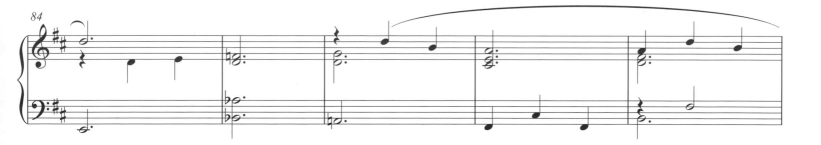

O Come, All Ye Faithful

Music by John Francis Wade
Latin Words translated by Frederick Oakeley

O Holy Night

French Words by Placide Cappeau
English Words by John S. Dwight
Music by Adolphe Adam

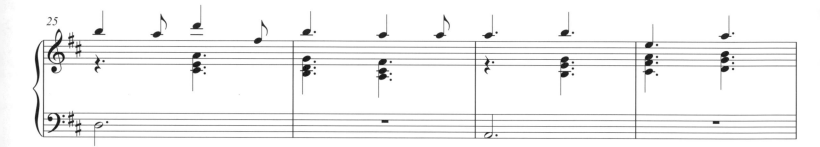

O Little Town of Bethlehem

Words by Phillips Brooks
Music based on Traditional English Melody

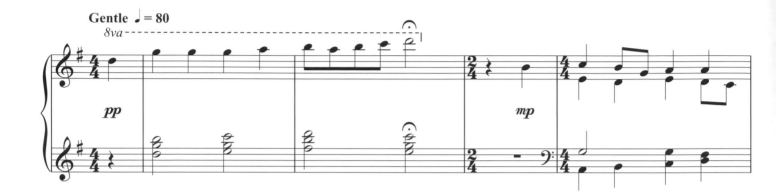

Once in Royal David's City

Words by Cecil F. Alexander
Music by Henry J. Gauntlett

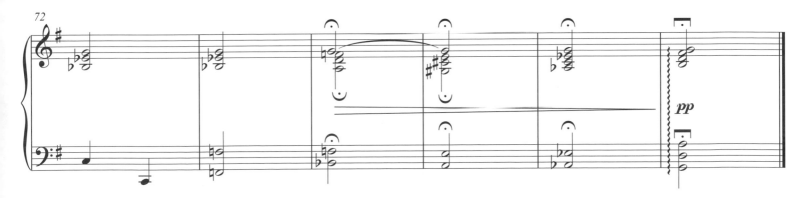

Silent Night

Words by Joseph Mohr
Translated by John F. Young
Music by Franz X. Gruber

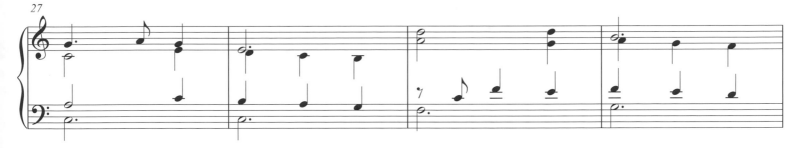

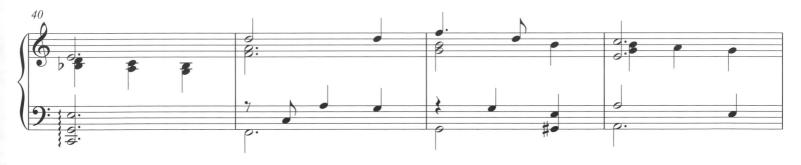

8vb⌟

Silver Bells

from the Paramount Picture *The Lemon Drop Kid*

Words and Music by Jay Livingston and Ray Evans

71

Walking in the Air

from *The Snowman*

Words and Music by Howard Blake

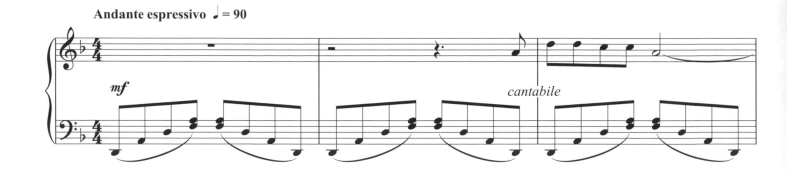

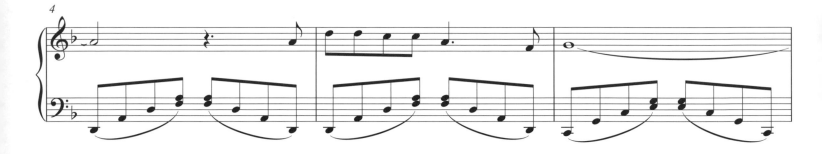

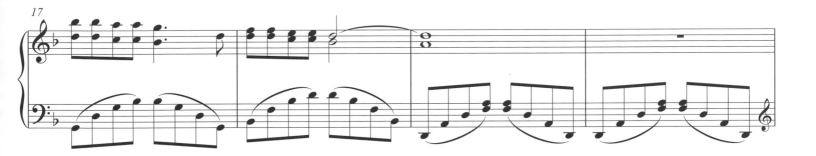

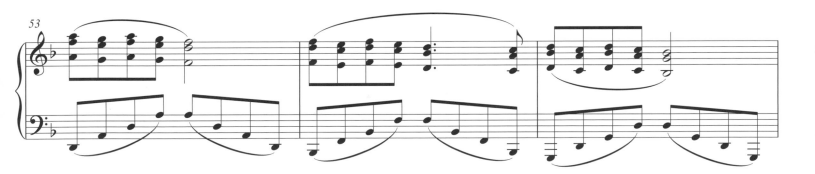

What Are You Doing New Year's Eve?

By Frank Loesser

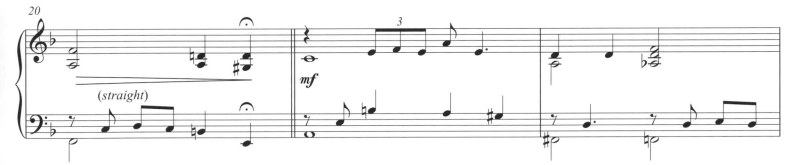

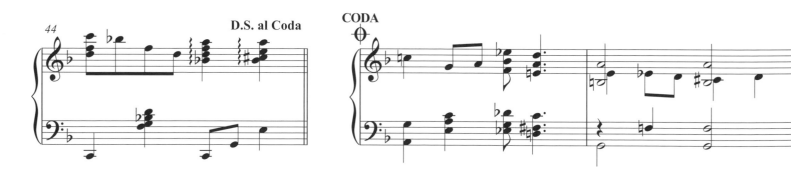

When a Child Is Born

Words and Music by Alberto Salerno, Ciro Dammicco,
Dario Baldan Bembo, Francesco Specchia and Maurizio Seymandi

Translated by Fred Jay

White Christmas

from the Motion Picture Irving Berlin's *Holiday Inn*

Words and Music by Irving Berlin

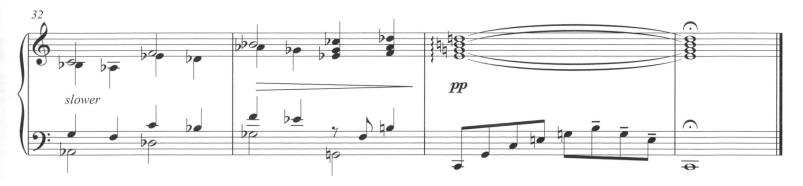

A Winter's Tale

Written by Tim Rice and Mike Batt

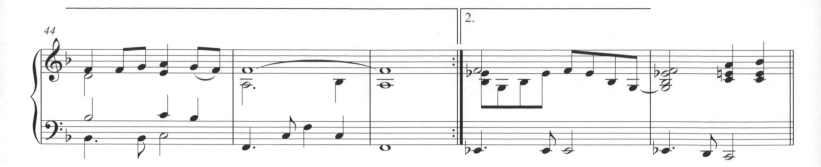

Discover the rest of the series...

ORDER No. HL00286009

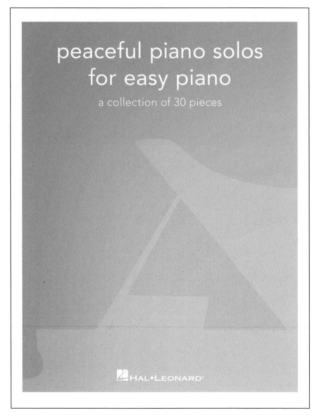

ORDER No. HL00286428